CITY OF FLOWERS

Memoir of a Teenage Traveler

Diane E. Greentree

CITY OF FLOWERS
MEMOIR OF A TEENAGE TRAVELER

iUniverse books may be ordered through booksellers or by contacting:

*iUniverse
1663 Liberty Drive
Bloomington, IN 47403
www.iuniverse.com
1-800-Authors (1-800-288-4677)*

*ISBN: 978-1-4917-4704-9 (sc)
ISBN: 978-1-4917-4703-2 (e)*

Library of Congress Control Number: 2014916847

Printed in the United States of America.

iUniverse rev. date: 10/29/2014

CONTENTS

For my mother and her grandchildren

It's okay to look back, even as you move forward.

—Jennifer E. Smith, *The Comeback Season*

ACKNOWLEDGMENTS

I would like to thank the Rotary Club for providing opportunities such as exchange programs for teenagers. To Alexis Easley's memoir writing class at University of Alaska in Juneau for starting me on this writing venture. To Kerri Buckley's freelance writer's course in Astoria, Oregon, for inspiring and sometimes cajoling me to follow through. To Pastor France Marcott for instigating a writer's club that met in the long, dark nights of an Alaskan winter to pluck away at something resembling a story. For my readers and their insightful observations and suggestions, especially Barb Revenig. To Katie Humphrey and her wonderful Rebel University for helping me regain vibrant health and reconnecting me with my purpose. And mostly to my loving husband, Charter—thank you for everything.

INTRODUCTION

I started writing *City of Flowers* when I was a single, professional woman with an advanced degree and a lot of personal freedom. I signed up for a creative writing class with the idea that I would finally put some effort into my long-held dream of becoming a writer. Secrets, it turns out, were just waiting to be unveiled.

Initially, I simply wanted to reflect upon and write about a fantastic experience. The notion of getting to relive aspects of that magical year abroad was exciting. So, it came as a complete surprise when the feedback from my classmates focused on who I was *before* going to the Philippines. What was going on in my life? What was so bad that I felt I had to escape by going to a completely foreign place? What did my family think? What about my mother? I was stumped by those questions, as I was in the habit of suppressing personal thoughts, especially those regarding the loss of my mother to cancer when I was nine.

Finding answers began to expand the scope of my story and to bring healing to long-neglected areas of my life. It also brought uncomfortable emotions and memories that warred with my long-term strategy of avoidance. Thus, I shelved the project.

Life quickly changed when my boyfriend became my fiancé, then husband, then father of our first child, all in rapid succession. The joy and stability of these changes allowed me to back away from the professional world and dive into the new and uncharted (for me) waters of motherhood. As Lynn Davidman wrote in her introduction to *Motherloss*, once she gained a certain stability in life, she was then able to tackle the research that her insightful book offers. So, too, once I gained a safe, loving, stable place in life, I was able to complete this project.

My hope is that by articulating the events of my early life, teen girls and young adults who have experienced the loss of a parent, or an ideal, or who have just lost their way, will be encouraged to try again and find their own *City of Flowers* with its redemptive qualities.

1) Grief does not happen all at once or in a neat, orderly fashion. When a child suffers a loss, she or he does not have the emotional maturity to fully process grief and will do so only in spurts as (and if) her or his emotional and cognitive development continue. For this reason, children often do not cry long, and they return to play and normalcy quickly, lulling adults into thinking all is well.

2) Peer pressure, being a very powerful force in a teen's life and usually quite negative, must be countered with worthwhile activities and attainable goals.

3) Teen bodies are increasingly sexual. Emotionally, however, most are not ready for sex. When I stepped over that line and was then expected to step over it again and again, my emotional intelligence was dumbstruck. Paired with breaking the specific goal I had made for myself, my self-esteem plummeted and left me lost and vulnerable.

4) It takes courage to recognize when something is wrong and courage to do something about it. It takes courage to make your own decisions and courage for parents to allow their teens to do so.

5) We all have a bit of "ambassadorship" in us; it is the ability to represent through our actions the best of our culture to others.

6) If you're going to go somewhere to speak for your country, know your national anthem!

Some names have been changed.

PROLOGUE

Fort Collins, Colorado 1978

It was a cool Wednesday afternoon in February, and as soon as the bell letting school out sounded, I bounded outside with a nine-year-old's enthusiasm, looking for my ride. I was excited about going to Rainbow Girls club. Instead of my friend's mom, however, I saw Dad waiting for me. *What is he doing here?* He never picked me up after school. *Why isn't he at work?* With annoyance, I wondered if he forgot about my meeting, and I bristled at this unexpected change of plans.

I dutifully got into the car, and once I was settled, Dad quietly said, "Your mom passed away."

"Oh," I replied. I did not know what *passed away* meant and quietly sat there in a state of confusion, trying to figure it out. Did he mean dead? Was mom dead? *No way. Moms don't die,* I reasoned. *My mom is not dead. Sure, she has stomach cancer, but that's temporary, right? Maybe she moved to a new hospital.* I was stumped, unable to comprehend his words, his presence, or his uncharacteristic silence.

Approaching our house, I saw cars parked in the driveway. *Strange*, I thought, but I did not ask why they were there. Dad remained quiet as we walked through the garage. Inside, many church friends and neighbors were standing around, and when the door opened, all turned and looked at me. One bounded over, swooped me into the air, and told me how sorry he was that my mom died.

Died. So that was it. As the reality of that word moved into my consciousness, time slowed, my stomach clenched, tears formed, my hands moved to cover my face as if to protect myself, and a feeling of abandonment hit me. I ripped free from his grip and bolted upstairs to my room, screaming at him, "You're lying!" Disbelief overwhelmed my senses. I slammed the door behind me, threw myself on the bed, and bawled. Normally a quiet, polite girl, I did not care that my noise was making the adults uncomfortable. I was mad, and I wanted them to hurt as I hurt. I hit the pillow and tore at the blankets and flopped about.

Then I heard knocking. "Come in," I croaked. That same neighbor who hugged me and gave me the bad news stood at the bedroom door and talked over my crying. I am sure he had many good and comforting things to say, but I heard none of them. I wanted him and everyone else to leave. I wanted to set the day in reverse, back to just before I saw Dad's brown station wagon at school. I wanted to go to my Rainbow Girls meeting, eat cookies, drink punch, come home, and do my homework, just as I always did. I did not want these people around or any interruption to my schedule telling me my life had changed forever, leaving me in a state of profound loss and fearfulness. How would I go on without Mom?

The next few days were a whirlwind of activity, with relatives showing up, neighbors bringing covered dishes, and repeated trips to the funeral home. For a time, getting to stay home and play with my cousins made it seem almost like a party. Strangely, I did not know what my brothers were doing; all I knew was I would not cry again. I had pleaded with God, yelled at him, bargained for her return, and cried and cried. It did not change anything, and crying, I decided, only made me feel worse. I shook off the feelings of sadness and resigned myself to be strong, as I was now the only girl in the family.

Once the funeral was over and everyone had left, Dad sat my brothers, Mike and Allan, and me down to listen to a tape Mom had made. She recorded it from her hotel room on Maui where she asked him to take her when she realized her cancer was terminal. We sat quietly perched on the edge of the bed, trying to connect to the sound of her voice, but it was weak, airy, and distant and did not sound like her at all.

"God, this is creepy," Mike said.

Allan and I nodded agreement.

Dad cleared his throat. "Well, maybe we should listen to it once a week for a while, anyway."

"No!" I said, "It's too weird. I don't want to hear that. That's not my mom!"

He did not argue. Instead, he told us, "She wrote a letter to each of you that you can open when you turn sixteen. If it's too hard to listen to the tape, I guess we'll just wait for her letters."

I liked the idea of getting a letter from her in the future, and feeling a little more hopeful, I nodded agreement and silently left the room with my brothers.

I returned to school. What choice did I have? School is a necessary part of life, and though Mom's life ended, mine did not, and I had to go on without her. I think a week had passed. When I walked into the fourth-grade classroom, my classmates stopped what they were doing and approached me to say hello. It felt so strange. Even the kids that I never talked to or who had never talked to me stood before me.

I was embarrassed, and one last boy finally walked up said, "Oh, hi, Diane. I didn't see you come in."

I snapped, "Gee, I thought everyone had seen me by now," then turned my back on him and sat down.

This attention was not welcome. I wanted a mother, and she would never be back. If she had not died, my entire class would not be knocking themselves out to pity me. My head down, I vowed not to stand out anymore—not then, not ever.

1—WE'RE MOVING TO ALASKA

Sitka, Alaska, July 1982

I heard the swish of Dad's corduroy pants as he bounded into the room, cheerily announcing, "We're moving to Alaska!"

He adjusted a pair of eyeglasses and a pen in the pocket of his long-sleeve plaid shirt, adding, "Isn't it great!"

"What?" I asked in astonishment. "Alaska! Are we going to live in an igloo?" I knew federal budget cuts had slashed his Colorado-based forest service job, but I never imagined we would have to actually move, especially to where we might have to fend off polar bears. A mountain man at heart, dad's excitement was infectious, and I began looking forward to a new adventure.

Mike finished high school and, taking his skateboard and guitar, left for electronics school in Arizona. Just Dad, Allan, and I set out for Alaska that summer.

Watching out the airplane's little window, I was mesmerized by the vast, snowcapped mountains and saw the shadow of the plane like a wavering firefly flitting across them. As we neared Sitka, I noticed dark expanses of water spotted with kidney-shaped islands. Then the Alaska Airlines pilot announced our approach for landing, and the plane jerked downward to leave me wondering, *What land?* I silently prayed, *Please, God, I don't want to die like this.* The plane bumped, the air brakes shot up, and the tires jolted to a stop. Beginning to breathe again and uncurling my white-knuckled fingers, I dared another look out the window. We had, indeed, landed only a few feet from the very end of the runway where there was water and huge rocks. After a slight pause, many passengers began clapping and cheering, and we joined in, relieved with the safe landing and relieved that, apparently, we were not the only ones who had worried about our survival.

Someone from the forest service met us and drove us a short distance to our new house. The air was damp, and it was drizzling lightly. I wished for an umbrella. Our host easily swung the door to the house open, apparently because it was not locked. He must have seen my surprised look. Laughing, he said, "You just came from *Down South*. You don't need to bother with locks around here."

Allan and I looked at each other and shrugged, then heaved suitcases inside and left Dad to joke about Reaganomics bringing us to Alaska. We dropped our luggage and rushed to see each room. Allan found the back door and opened it and quietly said, "Diane, come and look at this."

Woods, as far as we could see. Though there were two other houses on the same dirt road, behind our house was nothing but dark, wet woods. A strong pine smell filled our senses, and my skin grew sticky from unaccustomed humidity. It felt so foreign that I reached out and shut the door, turning back to the inside, happy to find that light switches turned on lights and faucets turned on hot and cold water, and that our new home did not resemble an igloo at all.

Within days of our arrival, Dad left Allan and me to fend for ourselves, as his new position required routine ten-day forays into the woods.

His job was to inventory the Tongass National Forest—literally, to count trees in the nation's biggest national forest. The Tongass is the largest temperate rain forest region in the world, spanning five hundred miles (an area equal in size to West Virginia), filled with islands, trees, streams, mountains, salmon, and black bears.

As he departed, we yelled to him, "Don't lose count!"

He responded, "Oh, I'll try not to. Be good." And he was gone.

At first, the constant gray of overcast skies and the screeching of eagles as they played among the giant trees overwhelmed us, and we stayed in the house reading books and competing in double solitaire. It was companionable and nice, relying on each other that way, but soon we grew restless and began exploring. Town was an easy mile-and-a-half walk, the first part through Totem Park. Giant Sitka spruce trees, some towering over one hundred feet, mingled with intricately carved totem poles throughout the park. Several ravens *clock-clocked* nearby, making the hair on the back of my neck stand on end, as I had just read about the *kushtaka*, sea-otter spirits that can take the shape of anyone or anything, including ravens. We hurried along, trying to shake an uneasy feeling, and, thankfully, the path soon turned onto paved sidewalks leading to colorful shops. The streets formed a V, making room for an old Russian cathedral in the center of town—a remnant of Russian America. We were hungry and looking for something familiar, like McDonald's, but discovered there was no McDonald's or any other fast-food chain. We settled for bagels from a local bakery and found the people we encountered to be welcoming. We soon began making friends.

School started in the fall, and Allan went back to Colorado to finish his senior year, living with a bachelor whom Dad had worked with. With mixed emotions, I watched him go, feeling the bond we experienced that summer quickly slip away, and yet it also felt somehow right. Our family had officially broken up, a progression that started the day Mom died. It was liberating in a way, like now all I had to do was worry about myself, and though I had just turned fourteen, I felt very grown up and proud for having adjusted quickly to a new place.

As the weeks passed, I walked everywhere and liked looking for shortcuts, usually by cutting through yards. When two girlfriends were coming over to my house after school, I suggested we try a dirt path I had noticed a few days earlier. We looked at the path, hesitating, as it only led about twenty feet before opening to a wooded area. Waving my hand in a northwesterly direction, I calculated that my house was, "Just over there, not more than ten minutes away."

Feeling adventurous, we set out. Within moments, our dirt path and any sign of civilization were swallowed up by soft, springy muskeg, and large, snowcapped mountains loomed nearby. A cocoon-like quiet enveloped us, interrupted only by occasional birdsong and the whispery sound of breezes through the leaves. Uncertain and jumpy, imagining every rustle was a black bear in waiting, we wondered whether we should retreat, but I insisted that the house was "just over there," and we continued.

The boggy, sponge-like terrain still held late-autumn flowers. Our sneakers quickly got soaked as we walked, jumped, and dodged water holes. Then I heard a scream; the girl behind me had stepped right into a muskeg pit and sunk to her waist. I turned and quickly pulled her out, but her jeans were soaked and muddy. She started shivering in the cool October air. "Hurry!" I urged, not knowing what else to do, and we continued hopping across holes. Ten minutes passed, then twenty, and a sense of panic was rising in my throat when, at last, we burst out of the trees and there was my house! We ran for the porch, stripping off our wet, mud-encrusted clothing, and rushed inside to get dry and warm. Sipping hot chocolate and feeling relieved and humbled, we started laughing, and I promised to be more careful about what shortcuts to take in the future.

As a high-school freshman, I was walking home from school, dreamily thinking about Ken, a cute junior whom I had a crush on, when a car approached and slowed to a stop. The passenger door opened, and there he was. Ken asked if I wanted a ride, but the car was full, and I started to decline when he patted his lap and said, "You can sit here." Blushing mightily, I climbed in, trying to suppress a nervous belch beginning in my sternum and working up my trachea. Ken feigned not hearing it. We drove around awhile, amidst lots of chatter and laughter, but I was only aware of the warmth of Ken's breath on my neck and the closeness of our bodies. Eventually, the driver let me out, and I resumed walking home though my feet felt like they were floating. Ken cheerily called out the window, "Bye, burpy!" Nearby, I heard a boom box playing John Mellencamp's "Jack and Diane" and silently changed the names to Ken and Diane.

We began meeting in other places like the swimming pool and the library. One night, at a babysitting job, Ken and his friends stopped by, and he came inside to talk to me. We held hands and kissed for the first time. Meanwhile, his buddy, a German exchange student, serenaded us with his guitar. He stayed about fifteen minutes. Shortly after he left, I noticed a shiny, new penny on the couch where we had been. I picked it up and held it close to my heart, which was beating rapidly, and felt a tingling in my hand from where we had touched. I pocketed the penny, considering it my good-luck charm.

Before arriving in Alaska, I understood we would frequently move with the forest inventory, yet I hoped Dad and I would get to stay in Sitka. My hopes were dashed, and I reluctantly told my friends I was going to Petersburg. Ken drew me in and held me close. As I cried on his chest, we promised to write each other and see each other as soon as possible. Though none of my friends had been there except to attend sporting events, they teased me, saying I was going to "Penisburg," and filled my head with rumors of lurid sexual activity and general bad behavior.

Slowly and reluctantly, I trod up the gangplank onto a ferry bound for Petersburg, Penisville, or hell; it did not matter, really. I was leaving the first place I had felt happy in since losing Mom. The M/V *Malaspina* navigated the waters of the Alaska Marine Highway at fifteen miles per hour as it passed stunning vistas of rocky shoreline buttressed by dark, mysterious forests, further back-dropped by endless mountain ranges. Seabirds scoured kelp beds, and eagles soared overhead. Occasionally, the ship's captain announced sea-life sightings.

I took it all in, then retreated to the solarium deck, where I lay brooding in my sleeping bag, set on a lawn chair underneath a heat lamp. The cold, crisp air brushed my face, and I twisted and untwisted the same lock of hair, willing the curl of my first permanent to remain.

I thought mainly about Ken and about the day not long before when I was passing the lake on my way home from school and saw people ice-skating. It looked fun. Rushing home, I grabbed a pair of ice skates and ran back to the lake. Catching my breath, I bent to put on my skates, and as I rose, a warm feeling of belonging swelled up in me, nearly knocking me over, much the way an oversized dog might topple its owner in welcome. Awkwardly trying to balance on thin blades, I fell just as Ken skated by. Helping me up, he skated with me. My chest tightened, and tears threatened to form as I sat there missing him and the sense of joy of that day.

But I refused to cry. Tears would not change the situation. Anger felt more powerful, and I decided to stay angry at Dad for making me start over, yet again. The sense of adventure I had fostered in Sitka changed to reluctance, bitterness, and unwillingness. I simply did not want to go.

Once in "Little Norway," Petersburg's actual nickname owing to its Norwegian heritage, my gloomy outlook continued. I quickly grew to hate the gossipy culture, the smell of fish permeating the air, and how every male over the age of sixteen had facial hair—and a lot of it. I disliked the sound of brand-new, oversized trucks blaring AC/DC music while repeatedly cruising Main Street. Driven by their proud teenage owners who purchased them with their summer fishing money, several were fated to be wrecked in drinking accidents. Mainly, I feared the remote wilderness surrounding the mere forty miles of road and the town of only three thousand people, many of them related. It seemed there was no alternative or escape.

2—Setting a Goal

Petersburg, Alaska, Winter 1982

Walking home from the post office where I went each day after school in hopes of finding a letter from Ken or any friend, I tripped on a pothole and dropped my good-luck penny. While retrieving it, I watched a pickup truck approach and slow beside me. Two boys were inside. The passenger rolled down his window to ask, "You wanna ride?"

"Oh, no thanks," I said, and kept walking, hoping they would go away.

The truck stopped, and, leaning far out the window, he asked, "Why won't you ride with us?"

"I just prefer to walk is all," I said. I knew these boys from English class but had had no interaction with them outside of school. I had no idea why they were giving me attention now.

The driver shouted, "Hey, I heard they called you *tight shoes* in Sitka. You're not in Sitka anymore, so you'd better learn to loosen up if you want to make it here." Laughing, they drove on.

Stunned, I stood there as their words sank in. *Tight shoes! Where did that come from? And how did they hear about it? And what does it mean? And what did they mean by "loosen up"?*

Disturbed, I walked the perimeter of the neighborhood until well past dark (about four in the evening), when it hit me: tight shoes meant that I had standards. Before meeting Ken, I dated a few guys and only let them kiss me and maybe put their hands on my still small breasts. Giggling, I felt proud to have such a distinction, but I soon grew scared as it became clear what was expected if I were to fit in. We were going to live in Petersburg two years, not a mere five months like Sitka. *Can I remain a virgin here?* The thought came tentatively, from somewhere deep, then again, with more strength: *I can remain a virgin.* As quickly as the thought crystallized, doubts began. *How will I have fun? Won't my friends think I'm too good for them? I'll be singled out and considered different.* Frustrated, I cast about for help. Then I remembered Mom's letter. I did not want to do something I might regret before even knowing what she had said, did I? With new resolve, I solidified my goal; I would remain a virgin in Petersburg.

Melissa and I were slowly cruising the three-and-a-half-mile loop around town in her maroon 1970-something Chevy Camaro, which she bought with her mother's help. Melissa, tall and pretty with dark brown hair and auburn eyes, had moved to town a few months before I did, and we quickly became good friends.

"Track practice was tough today. My legs feel like jelly," Melissa said.

I nodded agreement while stuffing a hot dog with chili into my mouth. "Uh-huh, Coach really pushes. At least it keeps us in shape."

"Hey, did you get a letter from Ken yet?" she asked.

I glanced out the window, noticing a gorgeous patch of pink fireweed in bloom, then slowly replied, "No, not yet." It had been three weeks since my latest letter to him. Changing the subject, I asked, "Do you want to go to the movies tonight? Maybe we'll meet some nice guys there."

"I hope so," Melissa said. "All the guys want to do around here is get into your pants. It's not like I'm a prude or anything, but shouldn't there be a little romance first? Why not bring flowers or something? Maybe then I'd be more open to groping," she complained.

"I know what you mean," I said. "It's like, 'Hey, wanna go out?' Then like, 'Hey, let's get naked!' I don't get what the big deal is."

We grew quiet, thinking about the continuous stories leading us to think nearly all of our high-school population was "doing it."

Just then we spotted Betty and Lou waving to us. They had a reputation for hanging out with the military guys in town. "Hey, Melissa, let's pick them up," I suggested.

"No way! I hear those two are so loose they'll go to bed with anyone. We don't want to be seen with them," she said.

"I know, but talking to Betty the other day about the history assignment, she seemed really nice. Besides, maybe she can tell us more about the whole sex thing," I said.

"Oh, all right," Melissa said.

Lou, with short, dark hair and a stout build, quietly said hello and slipped into the backseat. Betty, in contrast to her friend, was petite, had long, blonde hair, and chattered nonstop as she climbed in the car.

Betty said, "Hey, it's really cool you picked us up. Can you take us to the base? We're on our way to see my boyfriend."

Melissa and I exchanged knowing glances. "Sure, why not? Who's your boyfriend?" Melissa asked.

"Oh, he's just a guy. He's not around much because his ship is gone a lot, but when he's here, oh boy!"

"What do you mean?" we both chimed.

"Well, it's like sex with him is totally like a tornado, you know? I mean, the first time it hurt like crazy. Then after a few times, it got to be fun. And now, I can't wait to see him!" she gushed.

Then she added, "Hey, have you guys ever had sex? Oh, no, I guess not. Well, I don't know what you're waiting for. Everyone is doing it. People will think you're stuck up if you don't." Before either of us could reply, she said, "Here's our stop. Thanks for the ride!"

We were glad to let them go.

We sat there a few minutes, thinking about Betty's story, and then Melissa said, "Maybe we should put out. But I want to be in love first. What about you?"

"Oh, I don't know," I replied. "It just seems so casual. It's like we can't be popular if we're not doing it. That's wrong, isn't it?"

"Maybe, or maybe we're just being stupid," Melissa said.

I wanted to tell her about my goal and my mother's letter, but a heavy silence fell, discouraging interruption, and I asked to be let out at the corner to walk the rest of the way home.

As I walked, I thought about Mom's letter, the last tangible evidence of her, as her clothes and belongings had long since been given away. Somehow, we never talked about her, and memories faded with each passing year. I hoped her writing would tell me what to wear to always look great, give me stunning ways to fix my hair, suggest how to act around boys so I could find a good one, and advise which classes would make me smart.

While the letter held a significantly elevated place in my mind, it had already been six years. My sixteenth birthday was still over a year away, and I had real troubles right here and now. I really wanted guidance about what was right and wrong. And I badly wanted to fit in. Dad seemed so uncool that I did *not* want to talk to him.

Suddenly, the old anger I felt when Mom died bubbled up in my chest. I began to wonder if whatever she had to say would have any real bearing on my situation at all. I mean, what could she possibly know about sex and being a teenager? Besides, she was not here; she was never going to be here. Dad was gone too, off fishing in his little skiff, never even bothering to ask if I wanted to go because I had turned him down so many times. Wrestling with feelings of anger, abandonment, and guilt for thinking these things, my thoughts grew dark, and I felt my resolve to hold to the goal of remaining a virgin slip.

3—EVERYTHING CHANGES

Dad must have noticed the changes I was going through. One Saturday morning, clearing his throat, he said, "Um, Diane, I need to talk to you about something." He asked me to sit down as he nervously began. Rolling my eyes, I knew what was coming since we had done "the talk" before.

Interrupting, I said, "Dad, you don't need to worry. I'm not having sex."

He looked relieved but did not let it go. "Now, Diane, I'm really glad to hear that, but you have to realize you're at an age when this will become an issue."

No kidding, I thought.

He continued, "Do you have any birth control?"

"No!" I shouted. "Didn't you hear me? I'm not having sex."

"Yes, I heard you, but I still want to make sure you know what to do if you change your mind."

And then I did change my mind. One Saturday night, cruising in my current boyfriend's truck, curiosity, rebelliousness, or perhaps too many beers got the better of me, and I decided to give in. We went to a friend's house and staggered down the hall into a dark bedroom.

The door closed, and for a moment I panicked, my mind racing, *How did I get here? What about my promise? Just get up,* I thought. *Take those three steps back out the door and back to sanity and to my goal.* Just three steps. My body reacted but not away from him or from *it.*

Later, I took those three steps out and went to the bathroom. Beer caps and bottles littered the sink, and I cleaned them up and then splashed water on my face and finger-combed my hair. I searched my reflection for some noticeable change. There was none, but inside I felt a shift from simply being a curious, rebellious, grieving, confused teenager to something different, something more cunning, more mature, more alone. Those minutes together did nothing to fill the gap in my heart.

Ever efficient, the rumor mill spread the news; before the night was over, most everyone knew what had occurred. The following week, I pretended we were in love, but as we walked through the halls in school holding hands, I was embarrassed and disappointed with myself. I broke up with him before the week's end.

Some weeks later at a party, I was sitting on a couch, sipping a beer, and squirming uncomfortably from too-tight jeans. The noise level in the room grew incrementally as beer flowed. Several people were playing quarters on the coffee table and splashing beer on the floor and on old copies of *Sports Illustrated.* This party, like all the other parties, had begun after the weekly basketball game in whatever home was without adult supervision.

Often, that meant my house. Dad's job continued to take him out of town, and friends would find out, and word would spread. The first couple of times, it seemed cool, and I felt popular. My older brother had done this on occasion in Colorado, and so it felt familiar. Still, I sensed what I was doing was wrong and was scared of getting caught. Often, I tried not to let on that I was home alone. Word usually leaked out anyway, and parties developed with beer and drugs and teenagers. The following morning, I would clean stains, mop up vomit, change soiled sheets, and dump ashes and bottle caps, pouring myself into the work and hoping my efforts would somehow make amends. Dad would return a day or two later and beam about how clean the house was and praise me for being so responsible.

But on this night, it was someone else's place. Into my third beer and losing focus, a basketball player sat next to me on the couch and reached across my lap for a beer. As he moved, his hand brushed my breast, and he smiled. I did not say anything, and a moment later, he put his hand on my knee and gave it a squeeze. I moved my hand on top of his and picked it up and away from my leg, all the while trying to concentrate on what some nearby girls were saying. His hand moved back to my leg, and this time slid up my thigh. Pushing him away, I said, "Stop it!"

Frustrated, he blurted, "Why are you playing so hard to get? You gave in so easily a few weeks ago. Just who do you think you are?"

Stunned, I did not answer, but some deep strength ignited, powering me to get up and leave. I moved unsteadily toward the door. I buttoned my coat and began walking very fast, not noticing the cold as the noise in my head grew ever louder. Mom's voice, Dad's voice, God's voice (whom I had actively been neglecting) couldn't reach past that noise. I felt dizzy, unplugged, and unable to focus. Was this all there was? Sex without love? Where was respect? Romance? The noise heightened, and my pace quickened. *What do I do now?* How was I going to adjust to my new status of "fitting in"? Before, I was generally considered "hands-off," as if the kids in town knew my goal and grudgingly accepted it. It was too late to go back to my original goal, wasn't it? Was I now expected to do it with any boy who asked? I felt weak and stopped walking. That was when I noticed the northern lights dancing overhead. Hues of blue and green cascading so near I heard a hum. But even the sheer beauty of the aurora borealis was not enough to shake my funk, and I dropped my gaze and shuffled the rest of the way home. A wave of nausea washed over me, and I knew I had to get out of that town.

4—AN ANNOUNCEMENT
BRINGS HOPE

Winter was rainy, the nights were long, and the days overcast and grim. Volleyball season had ended, but I kept busy with cheerleading and an office-cleaning job. The weekend parties continued throughout town.

As I sat in history class, not paying much attention and passing notes to Melissa, an announcement came over the loudspeaker. The Rotary Club was sponsoring a contest to send one person from my high school overseas on a scholarship. The place would be determined after a student was selected to go. The person chosen would be an "ambassador of goodwill" to his or her host nation. At first, the announcement seemed so farfetched I ignored it.

But the idea tugged at me, whether walking to school, doing set-and-dunk drills, or washing coffee pots at my job. *Ambassador of goodwill …* words creating an image so lofty and exotic and so foreign to my present surroundings. I saw myself in a long, flowing gown, holding a wand and issuing "goodwill" (like a fairy godmother) to all those around me. Then the coffee pot I was cleaning broke, shaking me out of my reverie. Back from dreamland, I knew then I would strive for a new goal. Who cared where; anywhere had to be better than Petersburg. I got to work immediately on the application.

A couple of weeks later, when I passed the first phase of the competition, I jumped up and ran outside, waving the paper and shouting to Melissa, who was across the parking lot, "I did it! I'm in the final running. I'm going, well, I don't know where I'm going, but I'm getting out of here!"

"Hey, Diane, that's great," Melissa responded. "What do you have to do next?"

"I have to write a paper about why I want to be an ambassador of goodwill," I answered.

"Well, good luck. You still have to beat nine other people, right?" Melissa reminded me.

"Yeah, but I can do it. I better get started." And I ran home.

Encouraged by this early success and convinced that winning the contest was the answer to all my problems, I became very calculating. This scholarship was mine, and I pitied anyone trying to compete against me. This knowing was deep and quite startling in its intensity.

Tamara was a competitor. I caught up to her after cheerleading practice and began walking home with her.

"How's your application coming along?" I asked.

"Fine," she replied.

I started in, "I really want to do well. I really want to be selected. I think this is the best opportunity I've ever had. It can really open up some new doors for me. I really want to get out of town and start over again.

Oh, but you want that too, don't you?" I asked, smiling sweetly. "I'm sure you'll do just fine."

Tamara replied, "It sounds like this is something you really want."

"Oh, I do, more than anything," I said, smiling even more sweetly.

"Well, good luck then," and she turned down her road. Later, I learned she did not bother to submit her paper. Her desire must have paled next to mine.

Soon, I was one of the top three applicants at school, and all that remained was to prepare and deliver a speech to the Rotary Club. The day of the speech was a day of torment. A long burp started in the pit of my stomach and tried to move up my trachea to sing its way out my mouth.

The other two finalists gave their speeches and received polite applause from the Rotarians, but I barely heard anything as I concentrated on not burping. Then it was my turn. I swallowed and summoned all my strength to suppress the belch. Choking out the first few words, I paused and took a deep breath and then began to talk more smoothly.

I described how I was adaptable due to the many moves my dad's profession required, and how I could be mature in difficult times, having lost my mom six years before. I perceived being an ambassador of goodwill as a chance to showcase what is best in one's culture and to live my ideals without feeling pressured to do things I do not want to do. I think my cheeks grew a little pink at that point. I threw my heart into it, believing, perhaps, that I had found a way to regain the focus I had lost and to start again, and by the end of the speech, I was standing a little taller, and my blush had grown into a rosy glow of accomplishment. The audience enthusiastically applauded, and I just knew I would be selected to go.

But where? I envisioned a sophisticated coffee house in Brussels, a sidewalk café in Bonn, or a view of the ocean in Sydney. Dad and I poured over atlases and maps, and I dreamed of sipping tea in London, swashbuckling through Egypt, or climbing the steps of the Eiffel Tower.

About a month later, the principal of the school pulled me out of class to hand me a telegram, which read, *Your assignment is Zamboanga City, Philippines.*

Sam-bo-an-gah. Where the heck was that? I imagined a hot, muggy, buggy, jungle and felt a sinking in the pit of my stomach. This was not my plan! But I could not back down—not after being triumphantly selected. Not if it meant staying in this rotten town. I could not keep trying to fit in here. I needed a fresh place and a new start. Even if it was in a jungle, I had to go.

5—PREPARING FOR DEPARTURE

Information about Zamboanga City was sparse, but I did learn some interesting things in brochures the Rotary Club sent me. It included facts, such as: *"Population: 400,000; Local dialects: 4; Religion: Catholic, with a small Muslim population; Political situation: Stable, after the lifting of martial law in 1981 by President Ferdinand E. Marcos, put in place due to communist rebellion headquartered south of Zamboanga City."* Whoa, guerillas, rebellion, and multiple languages all in the same city—it sounded scary, exciting, and definitely adventurous.

About a week before leaving, Dad told me to invite friends for an early celebration of my sixteenth birthday. He cooked a lamb garnished with green-apple jelly and allowed each of us one wine cooler to drink. That was so cool! He gave me an Olympus compact camera. The flash screwed off, making it small enough to fit inside a shirt pocket. We tried it out, snapping shots of my friends, the lamb, and one of Dad and me. Its click was so quiet that we dubbed it my spy camera. Later, after everyone left, he handed me the letter and asked if I wanted to open it now or wait until my actual birthday.

I held the envelope and felt its soft, fragile edges.

Finally, here in my hands, was the other side of the story. The words my mother wrote a month before her death. Surely she would tell me about the trials of life. Maybe her advice was so strong I would never again give up on my ideals. A wave of guilt rushed over me as I contemplated what the contents might be, and the letter suddenly felt heavy. I tucked it into my Bible and, turning to Dad, said, "Thank you, but I think I'll wait a little longer to open this."

6—ARRIVAL IN COUNTRY

Zamboanga City, Philippines, June 1984

I staggered under the weight of the heat as I struggled to unbutton my blazer jacket. About twenty exchange students had traveled together, and we were chatty and excited on the long airplane ride. Now, walking in a daze, we cleared customs and made our way out of the airport, where we seemed to be enveloped by a mass of brown faces shouting, "Hey, Joe!" (a common greeting for a foreigner, taken from *G.I. Joe*). We huddled together and moved as one unit, until a Rotary official separated me and one other student bound for the southern Philippines from the larger group. We followed him to the domestic airport, nervous as each step took us farther from our group and everything familiar.

Hazy, heat-intensified scenes unfolded as we walked. A monkey's tail brushed my face as it rode on the shoulder of a boy who passed by. I gasped to see a boy across the street peeing directly into the road. I turned away and noticed wherever there were two or more people walking together that they held hands, even guys. I was shocked.

That night, I sat in a large kitchen at my host family's house. An overhead fan whirled. The sweet, sticky smell of cooked rice permeated the room. Several huge lizards scampered across the window screen, silhouetted by the inky blackness of night. Stifling a scream, I jumped when I saw them.

Laughing, my host dad, Uncle Joe, said, "Don't worry, geckos don't eat exchange students."

I wanted to believe him but still kept a wary eye on the lizards as he introduced me to his older sister, Lola, his daughter, Caroline, her cousin, Lydia, and several domestic helpers. Uncle Joe was a lawyer with a Princeton education and unattractive brown marks all over his bald head. Lola had a ready smile, white hair, and about eight teeth. She was dressed in a multicolored cloth that wound around her and tied in front. Caroline looked very sophisticated, with flowing, black hair reaching past her shoulders, clear, pale skin, and long, graceful fingers. On her blouse, she wore a black pin, a symbol of mourning for her mother who had died of cancer the year before. Lydia was twenty-seven and had an open smile and friendly manner. Just meeting her helped me relax.

The servants (servants!) prepared a meal of white rice and some kind of fish. I was hungry and ready to eat, but there was no dinner knife. Uncertain what to do, I watched the others push food onto their spoon with their fork. I awkwardly adopted this custom while trying to be polite and answer questions. Inside, however, I could not stop worrying about the geckos, and I tried not to stare at Uncle Joe's discolored head. It was hot, and I was so tired.

Finally, I was taken to my room. The door was solid mahogany, over eight feet tall, and carved with intricate floral designs. The houseboy, called "Boy," helped me drag my overstuffed, green, garage-sale suitcase through the door and heft it onto the bed. Cutting the rope tied around it to keep the contents in, I unzipped the case, and clothes tumbled out. Fatigued and irritable from the long journey and long day, I impatiently shifted past dresses, jeans, and T-shirts in search of my confirmation Bible, which held a picture of Dad, Mom's letter (still unopened), and a pressed flower from her casket. Exhausted, I placed these treasures on the desk and sat heavily on the edge of the bed. Boy told me where to find the bathroom, then excused himself and shut the door. Its solid thud gave me an unexpected sense of security, and I settled in for the night.

The next morning, waking refreshed, I had a much better outlook. I was once again thrilled about the adventure promised by my new surroundings rather than terrified by all the strangeness. Soon, I learned that Caroline and I would go to the same school, and it would be a university! (The Philippine primary and secondary school system finishes in ten years. I was in my eleventh year.) Breakfast was rice and mangoes. I was surprised to see rice again after having had it the night before, and I had never eaten a mango. Oval shaped and orange, it looked delicious. I picked one up, surprised at its weight, and admired the feel of its smooth skin. I was about to take a bite when Lola, laughing, took it from me and showed me how to cut it lengthwise. She did this twice, leaving a bit of space between cuts in order to remove a large pit in the middle. She gave me both halves and a spoon and showed me how to scoop out the meat. It was so sweet! I eagerly ate the pulpy goodness and was disappointed when it was gone so quickly.

It was time to register for classes. As I stepped through the heavy metal gate separating Uncle Joe's property from the rest of the city, I recoiled in shock. *Where did all of this traffic come from?* It was a cacophony of vehicles of all shapes, held together by rust and colorful paint, blaring horns, tires screeching, kicking up dust as they jockeyed for position, creating four or five lanes where there were only supposed to be two. Caroline handed me a handkerchief to prevent my choking and told me I should get some handkerchiefs of my own. The vehicles were mainly two types: jeepneys and tricycles. The jeepneys were akin to a trolley car and looked like rolling trinket shops, vying with one another for the brightest, gaudiest, most-cluttered decoration possible. Their benches were crowded with people sitting, standing, and hanging on for dear life. The most crowded even had people riding on the roof. I was relieved when Caroline opted for a tricycle, a motorcycle with a sidecar attached.

Along the way, we talked excitedly about the new school year, and I learned that she had been an exchange student herself in Pennsylvania. She was so pretty and sophisticated; I wondered if we could be best friends. About ten minutes later, the bike lurched to a stop, Caroline handed our driver the correct number of pesos (which looked like toy money to me), and we stepped onto the sidewalk.

7—A New School

Western Mindanao State University's (WMSU) expansive grassy areas and wide, windy walkways offered a welcome contrast to the noise and bustle of the city. The buildings were Spanish adobe construction, all ground level, with wooden-slatted windows, no screens, and arched doorways. Birds nested in the windowsills and sometimes flew into the classrooms. Large, flowering trees dominated the landscape and created generous shade.

As we neared the registration building, a crowd of people started in our direction. Within moments, a sea of indistinguishable faces formed a circle ten-feet deep around Caroline and me. Was a celebrity nearby? Why were they closing in on us? Questions began flying from the crowd. "What is your name? Where are you from? Why are you here?" The tones and accents, at first foreign to my ear, gradually grew clear. As I deciphered what was being said, it dawned on me, the crowd was there to see me. *Me! I was the celebrity.* Though I tried to answer questions, I really just wanted to finish registering. My eyes found Caroline and pleaded with her to get me out of the circle.

Seeing that I was shaken, she told me to get used to it. I was the only white girl in school, and my blonde hair and fair skin made me even more visible. At five foot six, I towered over most students, and at 140 pounds, I was much heavier than many. The biggest difference, however, was my nose. It is fully formed and, well, largish—something I had never previously noticed. I heard, "Look how pretty her nose is," nearly as often as, "Hey, Joe!" Shocked by the overwhelming attention, I clung to Caroline and began to think of her as a big sister, existing mainly to help me navigate this adventure.

I had a full schedule of classes. During the first week in Tagalog (the national language), the teacher asked students to come to the front of the class and sing the Philippine national anthem. Groups of four stood at the front of the class and sang, *Bayang magiliio por las ng silanganan* (land of the morning). That was the only class I shared with Caroline and the other exchange student, Tom, who was from Indiana. Since neither Tom nor I knew the Philippine national anthem, the teacher asked us to sing the United States national anthem. We walked slowly to the front of the room, looked at each other and, somewhat sheepishly, admitted neither of us knew the words. The teacher said,

"Okay, then sing any song you know."

I asked Tom what song he knew.

"Happy Birthday," he replied with a shrug.

We sang "Happy Birthday." The class laughed, but riding home in the tricycle, Caroline was quiet.

I asked what was wrong, and she blurted out, "That was so embarrassing! How could you not know your own national anthem?"

I did feel uncultured and naïve for not knowing the words but did she have to rub it in?

It was Wednesday morning, and I agonized over what to wear. "Civilian Day" came every week, and I was completely unprepared for its contest-like proportions. Girls dressed in their clingiest, most eye-catching attire, using the occasion to showcase themselves and their sense of style and catch the boys' attention. I had no sense of style and was happy to wear a standard white skirt, blouse, and shoes, as we did the rest of the week. One advantage, however, was I got to wear long pants, giving my legs a break from the daily onslaught of mosquito bites. In the first month, there were more than fifty bites per leg, just from my knees to feet. Eventually, the blood fest diminished, but there were never less than four or five welts at any given time. Given my lack of fashion sense, I was very surprised to be voted "muse" of the class. All the teams, classes, and social organizations had a "muse." And while I should have considered this title an honor, it mainly unnerved me. I could not remember anyone back home ever calling me a muse or telling me how lovely my nose was.

After school, I went to a nearby gym where I was learning to lift weights. I had learned to hail a tricycle and could get around freely. Waving my hand, I hollered to an approaching tricycle,

"Aqui! Aqui lang nong! (Here, right here, sir!)"

A brief look of surprise crossed the driver's face when he saw that he had an American for a fare. Then it quickly changed to a more expectant and somewhat wily expression, though he seemed friendly and chatty.

"How many languages do you speak?" he asked. "I speak six."

"Well," I replied, "I'm trying to learn Chabacano (the local dialect) and Tagalog and Spanish, but I really just speak English."

"Oh." He seemed to consider this, then added, "I guess I won't ask you to marry me, after all. I want a wife who can speak as many languages as me." He did not talk to me anymore.

Was he serious? Marriage? I wondered if I would need to use the phrase Lydia had taught me, *"No man po mo bah loco loco comigo! Bom bia yo combo!"* It means "Don't mess with me, I will kick you!" and is said in a threatening voice to wayward tricycle drivers or others as the situation warrants. Thankfully, this situation did not inspire fear, and he let me out at my destination without another word.

Since I had played volleyball in Alaska, I felt comfortable joining a team, though it was outside in the open sun. Returning passes was my strong move, and I scrambled all over the court, squatting and arms out, ready to return the ball to our spiker. The welts on my forearms, aggravated by humidity and heat, usually remained a long time after practice ended. Desiring to cool down, we rested in the shade of nearby trees and sucked the juice of chilled star fruit, a green, star-shaped fruit about the size of a lemon. It was citrusy but milder than an orange. It was better than a gallon of water. One teammate asked if I would come to the school cleanup that weekend.

"Of course," I replied.

On Saturday, I went on my own, as Caroline had other plans that day. Arriving at the designated time, I looked around and wondered where everyone was. Had I gotten the time wrong? Eventually, others arrived, joking about *Filipino Time,* and told me I needed to learn to arrive fifteen minutes late or more. We milled about, waiting for the organizers to get there. Some classmates greeted me and asked, "*Kumusta ka*! (How are you?) Can I see your hands?"

"Sure, I guess," I said, not certain where this request was leading.

They took turns holding my hands, turning them over and examining them, apparently expecting them to be smooth and pampered from a life of luxury. With puzzled looks, they dropped my hands and asked, "You know how to work?"

"Of course," I replied, surprised and a bit offended. I was about to tell them about working long hours last summer in a fish cannery, separating guts from roe, but thought it would be wiser to remain silent. Isn't that what a good ambassador should do?

"It's just that we thought, um, assumed, you came from wealth."

I could see their point. In all likelihood, none of the classmates I worked with that day would get to go to the United States, mainly for economic reasons, and partly for socio-economic reasons. Yet, here I was, a middle-class American with just A- and B-average grades, getting to travel and experience this generous and warm culture. What an opportunity! And what inequality. *It's so unfair*, I mused.

As we signed in, one boy asked me, "What is your middle name?"

"Elizabeth," I replied.

"Why didn't you include it when you signed in?" he asked.

"Well, I never use it," I said.

"Why not? It's a beautiful name. Is it a family name?" he asked.

"My mother was Mary Elizabeth, and everyone called her Beth."

"You dishonor your mother to not use your full name."

I had never thought of that.

Continuing, he urged, "You should have a logo."

"Why?" I asked.

"To personalize your signature. Your name was given to you. It's up to you to make it as unique as you are," he said. The others nodded agreement.

Intrigued, I asked him to show me, and for the next few minutes, several of us drew potential logos in the dirt with sticks. Soon, I found the right combination to form my initials into a symbol with one continual stroke. Excited, I drew my logo over and over. I did not expect to learn to value a part of myself that I had previously ignored or considered insignificant and to incorporate it into my whole identity—all by playing in the dirt.

Pictures Gallery

Mom (age 40) about a week
before she died (1978)

Newly arrived in Alaska,
14, and sporting my first
permanent (1982)

Sitka airport landing strip

Path through Sitka
Totem Park

Downtown Sitka with
Russian Cathedral

Ice skaters on lake
near Sitka

Petersburg coming into
view around the bend

Ferry approaching
Petersburg terminal

Aerial view of Petersburg

Fireweed field in summer

Northern lights

Dad in his fishing skiff

Kids working on jeepney

Street view of Zamboanga
City with lots of tricycles

Western Mindanao State
University campus

Another campus view

Volleyball team

School uniform with fan

Pig roast party

Walk to the park. I
am the tall one.

Turning sixteen

Relaxing with a cool drink,
friends, and pretty flowers

Location where Mayor
Climaco was killed

Funeral procession

Mayor Climacos's
final resting place

Military checkpoint

Looking somber at a rally

Notorious ice-cream
man at a rally

Overloaded bus

Nipa Hut in countryside

Water buffalo transportation

Children on the beach in the countryside

8—PARTIES

Reluctantly, I broke off a little piece of crunchy ear and nibbled it politely, but as soon as the hostess turned away, I spit it out and hid the remaining pig's ear inside my napkin.

I was attending one of many parties, but they were not the drinking fests I had known in Alaska. No, these were all about the food. And what food! At this particular party, eleven pigs had been roasted in an open pit for days and had apples stuck in their mouths as the final garnishment. Another feast featured an entire cow, spiked and roasted on turning spits for a week. And at one there was a whole tuna, about two hundred pounds, placed in the center of the table; it was probably the most delicious thing I had ever tasted. At every party, there was an abundance of white rice, fried rice, *pancit* noodles, fresh mangoes, chicken adobo, *dinuguan* (pork blood stew), sticky rice custards, and mounds of food for which I did not yet have names. Servants tried to shoo flies away from the tables with fans. All of the guests dressed in fancy clothes and jewelry. The women wore tailored dresses with lots of frills and lace and carried bamboo fans to keep cool. The men wore slacks and Barong Tagalog, an airy, embroidered, and untucked white shirt.

It was at such a party I met the famed mayor of Zamboanga City. Lydia told me that he was considered the maverick of southern Philippines. He wore his hair long to protest the practices of corruption and favoritism he believed shaped President Marcos's regime. He stopped cutting it in 1981 and vowed not to take shears to his head until the government withdrew its broad arrest and detention powers. Unlike many politicians in the Philippines, he did not travel in an armed motorcade, did not have a posse of bodyguards, and wore Barong Tagalog instead of western-style suits.

Across the room, I saw an older gentleman with white, shoulder-length hair and toes exposed above the plastic base of his orange flip-flops. He looked wild, like a windblown daisy, and out of place among all the well-dressed people, but his face glowed. I overheard him telling a woman a dirty joke and saw her blush. I grabbed Lydia's arm and asked, "Is that the mayor?"

She giggled as I backed away, tugging her along and hoping to remain outside his view. I felt nervous about meeting such a renegade and legend. But it was too late. He came straight across the room toward me. Uncle Joe was fast on the mayor's heels, and as they approached, he said, "Diane, may I introduce you to Cesar C. Climaco, mayor of Zamboanga City."

With an exaggerated bow, Mayor Climaco swept my hand up and planted a kiss on it, saying, "Welcome to Zamboanga, the City of Flowers."

Astonished by both his appearance and his courtliness, I stammered, "Thank you." He immediately moved on to speak with other guests.

Mayor Climaco did have one part-time bodyguard, Archelango "Archel" Fernando, who quietly appeared just then and offered his hand to me, issuing a shy, "Hello." I had not noticed him before but realized that he must have been in the room the whole time to maintain a watch on his energetic charge. Lydia later told me that Archel was a martial artist who could withstand a two-ton truck driven across his abdomen and two-by-fours broken across his forehead. In our brief exchange, I only noticed his engaging smile that suggested tenderness and warmth. He moved back to the periphery of the room with a catlike silence, but I was keenly aware of his presence from then on.

On my sixteenth birthday, my host family threw a party for me, inviting about thirty people, mostly family members, and there were three cakes! Though I had been in country only a month, I was feeling elated and buoyed by all the attention and the excitement of new experiences, if not by the tropical heat. I really liked evenings when it cooled off enough to sit outside. It was fun to tell stories of Alaska, describing the rain forest and mountains and explaining that it was not all Eskimos and igloos, though that is exactly what I had thought too, not two years before.

Once the last guest left, I thanked Uncle Joe for my party, excused myself, and went into my room. I had some business to attend to. With trembling hands, I carefully unsealed the envelope and read:

Diane,
Happy 16th Birthday! You are sweet
sixteen today, and I am sure as pretty
as you are sweet.

Dropping the paper, I could read no further. I had waited seven years, *seven years*, for this letter, this voice from beyond the grave, this wisdom from my mom. And with the very first line, she was wrong. I was not sweet, not anymore.

Fighting back a sickening sense of cowardice in the face of the courage that she had demonstrated in expressing her hopes for me while knowing she would not be here, I read the next line, which caused me to suck in my breath again. *I hope the last seven years have been good ones and the next eighty will be even better.*

Maybe she did have the wisdom I needed. This was the first time anyone had put words to the fear embedded in me that I would face the same fate of an abruptly cut-off life—and suggested that it need not be so. I began to breathe again, and as I read on, the simplicity and affection of her words seemed to whisper, "It's okay, you will make mistakes, you can try again, it's okay." I blinked back tears and continued, studying the handwriting, the tone, and the words. I tried to remember what she was like and wished she could tell me what my new life was about and whether she was proud of me.

She wrote about choices: dating, career, marriage. She encouraged me to try new things and keep up with old ones (like sewing). She told me not to let feelings like fear, anger, and resentment remain inside. If I felt them, I must acknowledge them but also let them go.

She said I should do the things I wanted to do and not be afraid of taking risks.

On one sheet of hotel stationery, front and back, her words told of her unconditional love for me. She required nothing of me, made no demands, and other than the part about negative emotions, did not give specific advice. There were no magic formulas, no detailed instructions, and no keys to happiness.

Seven years ago, she and Dad had returned home from Hawaii just in time to celebrate her fortieth birthday. She was in a bad mood that day and would not accept any presents. She was at home but in a rented hospital bed, and I had to sneak up to her room to give her a card my brothers and I had made for her. With a tear in her eye, she took the card from me. I wanted to talk to her, but she looked too pale and skinny and had lost most of her hair. Her appearance scared me, and I left the room quietly.

I continued reading the letter even as tears flowed freely and the words blurred. Caroline knocked on the door, and I asked her in. She saw me sitting on the bed, letter in hand, with my face red and blotchy.

"What's wrong?" she asked.

Crying, I reached out and hugged her. She politely listened, but her back was straight and her arms stiff as she held me while I blubbered about Mom's letter and my guilt. I told her I was ashamed of how I had acted in Alaska. Caroline sat with me awhile, but as soon as there was a pause and it seemed I could get control, she left. Later, as I walked past her room to the bathroom, her door was cracked open, and I saw Caroline kneeling at a makeshift shrine and burning incense to the image of her own deceased mother.

9—RELIGION, LOVE, AND CULTURE

Crossing campus, I had some time before the next class and wondered what to do when I saw a group of my Muslim friends sitting at a gazebo in the shade of a large banyan tree. I waved and headed toward them. I breathed in the fresh scent of azaleas from a nearby bush as I plunked my books on a bench and greeted my friends, *"Salam alaykum."*

"Wa alaykum salam," Ruth and Honey responded.

Then Ruth asked, "Why do you always walk alone?"

"Huh?" I said.

"You are always alone when you walk anywhere. Why don't you wait for friends to walk with and to help carry your books?" she asked.

"Well, I guess I just need to get to my next class," I said, a little puzzled over why my behavior would be questioned. I never thought walking alone might be considered strange, but from my first day in the country, I had noticed people always travelled in groups, often holding hands, even those of the same sex. At first, I

45

assumed that they were homosexual, but I eventually learned that it was well accepted and deeply cultural for members of the same sex to have a lot of physical contact (though it would be considered very inappropriate for a boy and a girl to walk hand in hand). Still, it seemed inefficient to wait for a group when I was perfectly capable of getting where I needed to be by myself.

Just then, Bong, one of the group, pointed at a pimple on my neck and, laughing, asked, "Is that for me?" I laughed too, liking the notion that pimples happened whenever someone was in love. At least it turned a source of self-consciousness into something nicer. But I saw a strange look in Bong's eye, as if his question was serious, and I unwittingly reached up to cover the blemish while shaking my head no. Then he handed me a letter. I did not know Bong well and recognized him mainly for his outburst a few days earlier when he vowed to "fight to the bitter end" should the war for Muslim autonomy engulfing the region affect his family. His comments followed in the wake of the news about a prominent Muslim, Abdul Alih, who was killed earlier in the week. Alih left behind eight wives and forty children. I argued that joining the fight would only exacerbate the situation, feeding a never-ending pattern of retribution rather than helping find a solution. I assumed this letter was a continuation of his argument, so I was not at all prepared for what I read:

> *Diane Dear,*
> *I know you just want to be friends,*
> *But my heart feels more strongly.*
> *I know that friendship can be the first*
> *step toward L _ _ _,*

Which is the first step toward marriage.
Yours very truly, Bong.

What! I was speechless. The others backed away, apparently knowing something about this. Bong stood up, removed his hat, and placed his hand over his heart in a gesture that looked very much as if he was about to confess his love for me, but I cut him off.

"That's ridiculous! You've only known me three months! Besides, I'll be leaving here in less than a year. Forget about it. Forget about me!" And I stomped off.

I was angry and confused. Though not the "wham, bam, thank you, ma'am" mentality of Petersburg, this type of attention went too far in the other direction. *What had I said or done to bring about such a proposal? How could someone suggest such a serious commitment based solely on passion?* It was no good to have sex without love, but it was equally wrong to have love without any relationship. It made me of think of that annoying Lionel Richie song, "Hello," that I heard everywhere—the dude does not even know the lady, but he loves her. *Come on.* Besides, I was only sixteen and not about to make a lifelong commitment to anyone.

The initial giddiness I felt from being part of a grand adventure was beginning to wear off, and in its place a more subdued sense of reality set in. I needed to remember to fill my pockets with coins for the barefoot children dressed in rags who followed me everywhere. I was supposed to get used to rice for every meal, a lack of fresh milk, and, worst of all, no chocolate! I had to accept that I would not see my dad again for a long time, or my best friend, Melissa, from home. I certainly needed to learn some Tagalog or at least some of the local dialect of Chabacano, rather than relying on everyone to practice their English on me. My first few months in the Philippines had been idyllic. Caroline and I acted like long-lost sisters. We went everywhere together, and she translated for me. I asked her about everything and accepted her replies as the final answer. But tension had been building between us, and shortly after the scene with Bong, Caroline and I had a big falling out.

I attended Mass with my host family each week, and afterward we went to their family gravesite. Caroline burned incense to the memory of her mother during a short ceremony in which she bowed three times and placed incense sticks on the tombstone. She asked me, "How often do visit your mother's grave?"

"Almost never," I replied.

"That's terrible! How could you be so callous about your mother's memory?"

"Well, I live in Alaska, and her grave is in Colorado. So, I really can't visit, can I?" I retorted.

"You should go, even if you have to travel to Colorado." She scowled at me, and our conversation was over.

On another day, we were both standing in front of the mirror in the bathroom, brushing our teeth. She used slow, delicate strokes for several minutes. I rushed and was heavy-handed. Finishing first, I grabbed a towel to dry my face. She pulled it back from me and shouted, "That's my towel! Don't ever use any of my things." And she stomped off. I couldn't think of anything to say, and we stopped talking.

In her place, Lydia became my close friend and companion. She thoroughly enjoyed her job as an accountant at a local department store. Sometimes I visited her for lunch. Upon arriving at her office, I called, *"Kumusta ka!"* and she responded, "Great, how are you?" Then leaving her old-fashioned typewriter with its three copies of crinkled paper with carbons wedged inside, we would go eat *halo-halo* (a fruit and custard cup) or another local delicacy.

One Saturday, we sailed with some girls and guys to Santa Cruz Island, one of the only places where it was permissible to wear a bathing suit in public. Sitting in the shade of a coconut tree and sipping San Miguel beer, the talk turned to the issue of marriage. Lydia, who had been with a steady boyfriend for several years, reddened a bit.

"Why don't you marry him?" I asked her.

"I would really like to, but marriage is such a heavy burden." She sighed. I thought about the young families we knew. Women spent all day washing clothes by hand, preparing food, and caring for babies, and they aged quickly, appearing much older than their given years. Modern appliances, such as washing machines and microwave ovens, were practically nonexistent.

"Besides," Lydia continued, "I would have to quit my job."

I knew what she said was true from the courses I was taking in school. The cultural norm did not account for a working wife.

The conversation hit a lull, and we went swimming. Splashing about in the water, I suddenly felt a sharp pain in my foot. Trying not to panic, I swam toward shore as fast as I could. I crawled onto the beach a safe distance from the water before I had the nerve to look at what bit me. I had stepped on a sea urchin, and its spine lodged in my foot. The others came running over, wondering why I looked so scared. When they saw it was just an urchin, they told me to calm down. They said ammonia would ease the spine out. Great. We were on a secluded beach. Where were we going to find ammonia?

The guys stammered, "Well, the best source of it is urine."

"Gross!" I yelled in disbelief.

But I dutifully sat at the edge of the picnic table with my foot propped up and waited to be tended to. The guys started guzzling beer. Each drank down a bottle, then went into the bushes to refill the bottle, and then poured the urine over my foot. The warm liquid splashed, easing the urchin spine out of my foot. One guy, David, drank beer after beer but could not refill the bottle. He said he had a kidney problem and he would be able to help me out soon.

"It's okay, my foot is feeling better," I said.

But he persisted and disappeared into the bushes. The others had lost interest and wandered off, leaving me to wait. I was a little embarrassed and drank a beer myself. I began to think maybe this was the kind of chivalry I was looking for—practical, not overly emotional, and rooted in finding solutions in a respectful manner, no matter how crazy the situation. It resembled my dad's reaction when he found out I was having sex. That particular conversation had been very hard. Dad had started talking and expected me to overreact to his suggestion I was having sex. When I remained quiet with my head down, he knew the truth. Though he told me I should wait until marriage, he tempered the advice with the reality of buying me condoms.

About forty-five minutes later, David returned to pour the warm liquid over my foot, and the cure was complete.

There were many subcultures within the Filipino culture. Several weeks after the Santa Cruz beach outing, I was invited to a different beach picnic. This one was with my group of Muslim friends who, thankfully, glossed over my abrupt refusal of Bong's attention. We were to meet at school and travel together, and I arrived fifteen minutes late, thinking I had really caught on to the way things worked. As I waited and waited, almost an hour passed, and I grew worried. Was there an accident? Where was everyone? Finally, they arrived, and off we went. Laughing at my concern, they explained that there is *Filipino Time* and there is *Muslim Time*. *Oh*, I thought.

When we got to the beach, I was hot from wearing a bathing suit under my clothes and was about to pull my T-shirt off when one of the girls told me not to. I looked around and saw that everyone was fully clothed, even wearing jeans into the water. I suddenly felt conspicuous for wearing shorts. Leading the way, my friends ran into the water, not seeming to mind their drenched jeans, and I followed. Soon we were tossing a Frisbee and splashing around and enjoying the day.

Back on the beach, the older women were preparing food. They were the families of my schoolmates, and there were many siblings, parents, cousins, aunts, and uncles, and I really did not learn anyone's name. Nor did I recognize much of the food, which seemed to be mostly small fish fried to a crisp. I tried a little bite and did not like the taste so I chose rice and a bright green, stringy salad that I was told was seaweed. The seaweed was delicious! I took a helping and ate it and asked for more. I must have had three helpings when I felt my stomach clench and I ran to the water's edge, losing my lunch in a most undignified way. One friend came to my rescue, sympathetic to my condition, and explained that "too much seaweed can have a diuretic effect."

"You mean I'm going to get the runs too?" I asked.

She nodded and helped me splash water on the throw up I had just made and said, "We had better get you to a bathroom."

As we trudged away, I am pretty certain I saw the aunts giggling.

10—Political Intrigue

I saw Mayor Climaco on a couple of occasions: once at the disco and again at a Rotary meeting. Each time, I had a chance to talk with Archel, whose calm and pleasant demeanor made me comfortable. I asked Archel if his job was difficult. He replied that it was challenging to keep up with the mayor, who insisted on doing many things on his own despite the inherent dangers. Newspapers were filled with reports of uprisings, murder, and political misdeeds. President Marcos, who was sick, seemed to be losing his grip on power. Armed checkpoints speckled the city. They stopped jeepneys and tricycles to examine people and ask questions. As we talked, Archel looked at the sign-in roster to inspect the logo I now used as my signature.

"That's really nice," he said, and he pointed it out to the mayor when he came over to sign the roster.

Climaco said, "Ah, you are blossoming into such a beautiful young woman, right here in the City of Flowers."

In the early morning hours of November 14, 1984, the mayor rode alone on his motorcycle to check on a fire that had burned down a business overnight. Just as he was getting ready to leave the site, a gunshot sounded. He fell with a bullet lodged in his brain; he was dead. The gunman escaped through a nearby alley.

It was Lydia's birthday, and we were preparing *siopao* (steamed, meat-filled buns) for her party when we heard the news over the radio. All chatter stopped, and the room grew silent. Lola started weeping softly. The servants disappeared into the courtyard. Lydia sat down and shook her head. How could this happen? Everyone loved Mayor Climaco. Who would kill him?

The funeral procession started at the church where he attended Mass and continued a little over a mile to a park named after him. Over half the city showed up, creating a sea of yellow T-shirts (the mayor's favorite color) and carrying flowers and candles. The people slowly proceeded to his final resting place. I was caught in a human wave, moving along the dusty streets with sounds of sobbing and moaning resonating from the crowd. The pallbearers were dripping sweat as they carried his coffin. A nearby pocket of foreigners moved with the crowd, forming a circle by linking elbows to stave off the crush of mourners. They were reporters from *Newsweek* and other publications, there to cover the story of Zamboanga's beloved leader. I kept my distance, somewhat affronted by the intrusion of foreigners and forgetting I was one myself, as I was so caught up in the grief and the injustice of the murder.

There was another feeling present too. It was one of empowerment and action. It was a sense that an injustice could be made right through the collective will. The funeral procession began to take on the feeling of a political rally as the slogans, "Down with injustice!" and "Martial law must end!" began to mingle with the mourning cries.

Momentum built, and within days of Mayor Climaco's burial, rallies were taking place all over the city. Those things he stood for in life, such as compassion for the poor and restoration of human rights and dignity, became the mantras of his followers. Swept up in the mood, I attended the rallies and sometimes took the stage to add a word or two of my own. This sense of political involvement and awareness was new to me, and it was exciting. I had never given a political speech, attended a rally, or publically voiced my opinion, and it felt good.

Late one Saturday evening, I was leaving a disco with Lydia and several friends when we were stopped at an Active Counter Terrorism (ACT) checkpoint by armed military. Since the mayor's death, the military patrols had been doubled, and M16-toting soldiers seemed to be on every corner. After checking our identification and winking at Lydia and me, they let us pass. We went to a late-night café where we sipped mango milkshakes and talked.

"The newspaper says it was Alihs who did it," I said.

"Why would the Alihs kill the mayor?" Lydia asked.

I mockingly recited the article I read, "'As an act of retribution for Abdul Alihs death,' *of course*." The Alih's were one of several large militia families in the region fighting for autonomous rights as Muslims in this Catholic-dominated country. I continued with the report that "Perhaps Mayor Climaco had ordered Abdul's death, so his brother, Rizal, avenged him."

Looking at each other, we began to laugh.

"Yeah, that's what happened. Mayor Climaco was really in the business of execution," Lydia answered sarcastically.

Our voices dropped as we spoke of what we really thought had happened. A month earlier, a mayor in a northern city was murdered in an eerily similar manner as Mayor Climaco. That mayor had also been known to be critical of the president. Marcos's health was failing, and there seemed to be a lot of effort to make him appear strong and in control by the federally controlled media. We dared not speak too loudly of our suspicions about the mayor's death. We believed his murder had been encouraged by the president as a means to stop dissent. It was not the kind of democracy I knew at home.

11—THE BARRIO

"Hello? Is it me you're looking for?" a boy in a passing jeepney loudly sang as Lydia and I waited for a bus to take us to her family home in the country. I rolled my eyes and waved to the boy. Enthusiastically, he waved back, one arm holding onto the vehicle and the rest of his body leaning into the breeze.

Boarding our bus, we squeezed next to an old woman with a chicken coop on her lap. It was so crowded that some people rode on the roof. The crowds did not matter to us because we were headed to Patalon, a country barrio twenty-seven kilometers south of the city. It was Christmas break; we were excited and ready for an adventure.

Her house was built on raised bricks and had a shingled roof. This was in contrast to the neighboring *bahay kubo* or *nipa* huts made with bamboo walls, palm-thatched roofs, and sitting on stilts. There was no electricity, yet it was comfortable due to its raised design and well-placed windows that allowed pleasant breezes to circulate.

After dropping off the backpacks that contained a few changes of clothes, we decided to walk along the dirt road so Lydia could show me around. Soon, we saw a water buffalo lumber toward us. It was pulling a cart that held a large wicker basket and a lady sitting serenely on its back while her child rode in the basket. With a gleam in her eye, Lydia ran across the road to talk to the lady. Before I knew what was happening, they were unhooking the basket and preparing to push me up onto the beast's back. The only large animal I had ever ridden was a very tame horse in summer camp when I was twelve. This animal was much bigger than a horse. With trepidation, I let them push me up, trying not to show fear. Once I was situated, I felt like a terrified little kid at an amusement park, only this ride was alive and so big that my feet stuck out to the side. It grunted beneath me. The strange lady and Lydia prodded it to move, but the animal must have known it had a novice rider and did not care to go. What it did want to do was sink into a nice, deep patch of mud, taking me with it. My feet were nearly stuck before they grabbed my hands and pulled me to the safety of the road. They were laughing so hard they almost fell in the mud themselves.

Up the road, some neighbors asked us in for a cup of *tuba*, or Filipino wine, a fermented beverage made of coconut sap. I was advised to drink just a little, as too much could quickly affect senses and sanity. To extract *tuba*, a *coconut pilot* shimmies barefoot up a coconut tree, lops off the end of an unopened coconut bud, and gathers the sap. It is then fermented for several days. Our host pointed out the tree that our toddy came from, and, noticing that it was very tall, I asked if it was hard to climb.

"Of course not," our host replied, and asked if I would like to try.

"Sure," I said. It sounded like fun, and I was feeling pretty good from the drink.

A short tree was located nearby, and I tried jumping to get onto it but quickly found that did not work. One guy cupped his hands together and told me to step on them. More neighbors came to watch. I stepped into his hands, and he boosted me up, but I could not find my balance and fell back. Another guy offered to push me up the tree. I stepped back onto the first guy's hands while the other positioned himself under me to prop me up. I toppled down, bringing them both with me. A neighbor lady from a nearby *nipa* hut was crying from laughing so hard. I sat on the ground, dusty, sweaty, and defeated. The guys looked relieved when I announced that I gave up. Then one easily shimmied up the tree, knocked down three coconuts, deftly whacked them open with a machete, and handed them to us to drink.

At our house, we rested during the hottest part of the afternoon; we napped on woven mats set on wood benches. In the evening, we got ready for a barrio dance by pulling on dresses, combing our hair, and giggling with excitement. Paper lanterns lit up a dirt space, which was the dance floor, and music was played from a boom box. Each girl was given a glass jar for the boys to drop coins in for the privilege of a dance. The novelty of getting to dance with the American girl must have been great, as my jar filled quickly, but so did the jars of several others girls. I did not know it, but we were in competition, and the one with the most coins at the end of the evening got a prize. I won; the prize was a chicken. Lydia was happy and said we should cook it for dinner the next night. She asked if I would make it into an American meal.

"Sure," I said, "that's easy. We have chicken all the time back home. We'll just add mashed potatoes and salad."

The next day, Lydia and her family got to work. Her mom killed and plucked the chicken. I boiled potatoes, but when it was time to mash them, there was a small problem—no milk and no electricity or electric beater. We made do with a fork and powdered milk. I wanted to start making a salad, but Lydia shrugged and said, "There's no fresh lettuce or tomato." We substituted canned carrots. The meal was just about ready when I noticed Lydia and her mom hovering over the stove as if they were concealing something from me.

"What is that?" I asked.

"Rice," Lydia confessed.

"Rice! I thought you wanted an American meal. We don't eat rice!"

As we sat down to eat our rice, hard, lumpy potatoes, canned carrots, and fresh chicken, I thought how happy I was to get to try new and challenging things, even if I was not very successful. We all enjoyed the experience of sharing cultures and friendship. At that moment, I thought it was the best meal I had ever eaten.

The next morning, I was on the front porch making a large star out of scrap wood and colorful paper, when an ice-cream man on a motorcycle drove up. *Odd*, I thought. *Why would the notorious ice-cream man be all the way out here?* I called Lydia to look, and she raised her eyebrows when she saw who the visitor was.

I had often seen this man in town. He always seemed present at the rallies, but I had also seen him nearby when we would go to the park. Archel told me he was notorious because he was suspected of being a spy for the government. It was peculiar he should have a motorcycle and real shoes while all the other ice-cream vendors had push-carts and wore flip-flops.

He came up the driveway and asked if we wanted ice cream. Lydia bought several ice-cream sandwiches while I snapped a few pictures of him with my spy camera. We both felt relieved when he drove off. I asked if she thought he was trailing us; she shrugged.

A few days later, we were waiting for the bus to take us back into town when a new-looking jeepney barreled around the corner. Upon seeing us, the driver abruptly stopped, and three men got out to ask if we wanted a ride. Instinctively, we took a step backward and picked up our bags. At that moment, the bus arrived, and we ran toward it, waving our hands and hollering for it to stop. During our escape, we shouted, "Thanks, but no thanks!" and got on the bus.

When we caught our breath, I asked Lydia if she knew those men. "No, I've never seen them before," she replied. It was odd to see strangers and a nice vehicle in the countryside, and we felt uncomfortable.

I never felt scared for my safety during my months in the Philippines despite the constant news of killings and kidnappings. A few nights after returning from the country house, I was walking through Mayor Climaco's old neighborhood and heard a vendor calling, "*Balut! balut!*" (a boiled duck embryo). I walked toward him, curious about that prized delicacy, and noticed a beautiful parrot sitting on his shoulder. The vendor told me the bird belonged to the American journalist recently kidnapped and that he was caring for it until his return. Then he pushed the box toward me and asked, *"Balut?"*

"No," I said, wondering if these embryos had incubated too long and might cause customers to have to pick feathers out of their teeth. Hurrying away, I remembered to add a polite *salamat po* (thank you).

As I walked home, I reasoned with myself that I did not go places I should not, as some said that reporter did, so I could not be a target myself. But the recent sighting of the questionable ice-cream man followed by those unidentified men in the country gave me the creeps. I started locking my bedroom door at night and placing a piece of furniture in front of the doorknob, often lying awake and imagining that every sound was someone coming to get me.

Not all night sounds were frightening. Most homes had slatted windows for airflow, and you could often hear conversations in other houses. One night, the neighbors were singing a rousing round of Mayor Climaco's personal song. In keeping with his sense of humor, the verses contained self-ridicule that he made up himself. I smiled as I heard:

"Ay-si Cesar, Ay-si Cesar, Ay-si Cesar Climaco, (Look at Cesar, Look at Cesar Climaco!)

"Da'an guapo, y bien macho, Ay-si Cesar Climaco! (He's so handsome and so macho, look at Cesar Climaco!)"

I had never met a person as unique as Mayor Climaco and was glad to have known him, even for a short while. I hoped I could always remember to laugh at myself and be as caring and purposeful as he was.

12—A New Year

"Three-two-one, happy new year!" Shouts and clapping and fireworks and gunshots marked the first few minutes of 1985. Yes, gunshots! Most people could not afford fireworks, but bullets were cheap. Every year, someone was hurt or killed from weapons being discharged randomly into the air. A bullet had torn through the kitchen ceiling of my host family's home. Thankfully, none of us were in there.

It was after midnight, and I was drowsy from our feast and feeling giddy from the kiss of a cute boy. It was a quick, pleasant kiss, the first and only during my year abroad. I lay on my bed feeling refreshed and happy. It began to dawn on me that this was what Mom meant by *sweet sixteen*—a lingering sense of innocence and wonder, knowing full well that the responsibilities and privileges of adult life were coming. I felt content to let them wait a little longer. As I drifted off to sleep, I understood how lucky I was to experience my teens in this way.

Because of its proximity to the equator, winter does not exist in the Philippines, but the weather had grown cooler, and one morning I woke shivering. The radio announcer said the high temperature would be 75°F. And I was cold! I really had gone native. I dug through my wardrobe to look for a sweater, hoping it would still fit. Many of my clothes were now too small. Later, at school, I grew hot and gave my sweater to a friend. I was startled by a wave of homesickness caused by the comforting feel of the warm cotton against my skin, a sensation that I did not realize I missed until that moment. I decided to call Dad. We had not talked since I left, though we regularly exchanged letters, using thin, crinkly airmail stationery. It took me several attempts to dial the right combination of numbers before I got through.

"Hello? Hello? Dad! Hello?" I shouted into the mouthpiece.

"Hello, is this Diane?"

"Dad, it's me! How are you?"

"Diane, I'm well! Where are you?"

We did not talk long, maybe ten minutes. The satellite relay was sluggish and our conversation disjointed, so we ended it with a promise to write more letters.

Sitting at the kitchen table with my next host family, two middle-school sisters and their mom, laughing and talking about our day while eating fried bananas and sipping Coca-Cola from glass bottles, I felt a warm sense of belonging. I had begun an after-school judo course. I relished describing to them how a boy, twice my size, came toward me, and I grabbed his forearm with my left arm, pulling him in close, slipped my right arm around his back, and using my hip to shift him off balance, threw him to the ground. Then, of course, I extended my hand to help him up, and we bowed to each other, tightening our belts and straightening our judo gis. The sisters were impressed.

Later, after their dad was home and we had supper, the family went into the master bedroom to watch a movie. They invited me to join them, but they looked so cozy and cohesive as a family unit, all snuggled up on the bed, that I suddenly felt like an intruder and excused myself. I went into my bedroom and locked the door.

I brooded over the short conversation with Dad as I sat on the edge of the bed, my lower lip trembling, and I wondered why it was so hard to talk with my father. Then I began to remember my mom and a time she and I sat perched on the edge of a bed. We were laughing and talking about nothing when she suddenly got serious and reminded me that she needed to give me a spank from an earlier infraction. I had hoped she had forgotten. I was nervous as she readied me to receive my just punishment. Then she just did a slight tap on my bottom and laughed and said, "Okay, that should do." *That was it?* I was so relieved, and we laughed and hugged and felt close. The tenderness of that memory reached across all the years and miles to touch me and melt my defensiveness toward Dad. As I fell peacefully asleep, I resolved to write him the next morning.

13—GOING HOME

My final host family lived in a suite of rooms at the top of a hotel they owned. They were Chinese, and the immediate family was small, with just one nineteen-year-old girl living at home. They operated in an extended family system, however, and meals were prepared in a kitchen shared with my host father's siblings and their families. I often went with my new sister to pick up the food and carry it back to our place. I usually did not recognize what was being served and found myself picking at a plate of octopus bits and rice, listening to the family banter with each other in Chinese. My mind wandered toward home. I daydreamed about sharing my adventures with old friends, who would also feel transformed. My busy life slowed down; I no longer attended rallies, and finals were complete. I found myself emotionally withdrawing.

Then the Rotary held an exchange student conference. A group of girls who had been stationed together in the same city showed up and rocked my world. They knew each other well, and over mango milkshakes, they joked and bantered and talked so quickly it was hard to follow. I was dumbstruck. I had not heard the use of English in any way other than the most straightforward for almost a year. I had learned to speak very slowly and directly to be understood and to be comfortable understanding only about half of what was said. I had completely forgotten about nuances. Over the course of the three days we spent together, we laughed and talked and laughed some more. I soaked up their wit and humor and tried to bring my own English back up to speed, but when I could not follow the tone or innuendo (which was often), it did not bother me. So what if I was out of touch with my own culture? I began to understand that it no longer mattered to me if I did not fit in.

During the days leading up to my departure, I felt suspended, not sure where I belonged. The adrenaline and excitement that had propelled me through the past year began to dissipate, and I grew agitated and impatient, feeling the heat more keenly and the dust more deeply. I was uncertain what awaited me in Alaska.

I was really looking forward to seeing my dad and for the travel we had planned to see his sister in Australia. Beyond that, I could not picture what home looked like or imagine how much I would miss the Philippines. Would I miss the attention? My classmates? Lydia? The comfort of living with an intact, caring family? Would I miss hailing my own tricycle or squeezing into an overcrowded jeepney? I would certainly miss the tropical fruit. Would the sense of adventure and wonder translate to my own world, allowing me to see it with new eyes and a new attitude? In a year where it had been impossible to fit in, I had lost that deep desire. Would I want it back?

The transition came in pieces, starting with my dad meeting me in Manila. It was so good to see him but awkward too. I was so acclimated to the humidity that I completely forgot to turn a fan on for him and left him with a hot, sleepless night. I also failed to warn him that the shower stall contained a trashcan filled with water and a ladle was used for bathing. The faucet itself only provided the slightest trickle, not even enough for rinsing.

We flew together to Hong Kong, where we stayed a few days, en route to western Australia. He splurged for a nice hotel, and when I walked into the room, the cold air-conditioning took my breath away. I turned it off and opened a window. Outside, people were practicing tai chi. I went to the bathroom and turned the faucet on. Water! And plenty of it. I ran my hands under the flow, luxuriating in the silky feel, toggling from hot to cold to hot again. So this was how a faucet was supposed to work.

Dad and I toured Hong Kong, taking a city tour on a bus that was clean, modern, and without roosters. At one restaurant, we were seated at a large, round table with other patrons who noticed our awkward handling of chopsticks. One gentleman dressed in a business suit demonstrated to us how to hold the sticks while the others watched with amusement.

We talked about little things: how to hold the chopsticks, what we should shop for. I hoped for a new watch, and Dad was looking for a suit. The big things, the life lessons, had to wait. Time would tell how much my year as an ambassador of goodwill had matured and redeemed me. For now, it was enough to just be experiencing something new and exciting together before returning home to launch into life.

Back in the United States, I spent a couple of days with a friend from Petersburg. She invited some boys over. She wore a tight-fitting shirt, thick mascara (which promptly smeared), and makeup two shades too dark. I skipped the makeup and enjoyed wearing jeans for the first time in a year. The boys arrived, high-fiving each other and telling crude jokes, both wearing khaki pants and combat boots. *Odd*, I thought. We got in a car with them. The first stop was a convenience store where they bought candy bars, chips, and soda. In a daze, I looked at the rows of junk food, shocked by the amount and variety of sugar. Before the Philippines, I had been addicted to chocolate and bought a candy bar every day. After a year, when the price of a candy bar could feed an entire family for a day and chocolate existed only as a rare treat, I found I had lost my appetite for American junk food. I purchased a bottle of water.

"What's wrong with you? You don't eat?" one of the boys said to me.

I shrugged. I sensed that they would not wish to hear about judo. That they probably had never heard of a mango. Did not worry about insurgencies or fighting off mosquitoes. Would not care to think about impoverished children who approached me daily and wanted whatever I could give, whether a coin, a handkerchief, or just some recognition. That I had been proposed to more than once; ridden a caribou; experienced a political awakening; learned the names of food, plants, and animals I never knew existed; loved rice for breakfast;

and dreamt in another language—it was of no interest to them.

"You don't talk either?" the same boy said. Not waiting for an answer, he shoveled his food in as fast as possible, then pulled on a camouflage jacket and ball cap, pulling the brim down over his eyes. Similarly outfitted, his friend had his arm wrapped possessively around my friend's shoulder, and he opened the trunk of the car to retrieve a stash of toilet paper.

"Here," he said, pushing a roll at me. "You can start with that house."

You've got to be kidding me! They're planning to TP a house! God, will this evening ever end? I looked at them and shook my head no, then rolled up the window and turned away. I stayed in the car and sipped my water. Perhaps when they finished their mischief and came back to the car, they expected to find me fuming or pouting or upset. Instead, I sat contentedly, thankful for the memories and the sustaining gift the City of Flowers had given me—to make my own choices despite what others might think, to be myself without fear of rejection.

EPILOGUE

As Thomas Wolfe wrote, *you can't go back home*, so I felt in returning to Alaska. My brothers were gone, Mike working in California, Allan attending college in Montana. Dad had moved to a new town while I was away. My friend Melissa was living with her boyfriend. The dream of describing my experiences to old friends to excite and transform them soon dissipated. Instead, commonplace concerns like finding a summer job and taking correspondence courses to catch up on English and math claimed my attention. When I finished high school a year later, I enlisted in the United States Coast Guard (USCG).

A couple of years into the enlistment, I was visiting relatives, and I made a remarkable discovery. It was a book that had been given to my mom in 1945 by her second-grade Sunday school teacher. The book, *Patty Lou in the Coast Guard* by Basil Miller, was just one of a series of Patty Lou adventure books written in the 1940s. But it was the only one Mom had.

What was so special about that story? I read it and learned that Patty Lou was a motherless teenager with courage and faith who had been to the Philippines. She was also a Coast Guard Auxiliarist with her own boat and crew. I wondered what my mom thought as she read the story decades earlier and whether she dreamed of such a life for herself. I also wondered about the similarities of Patty Lou's adventures, which would have been considered unconventional at the time they were penned, and how the events of my own life played out. *Was she somehow guiding me?* I remembered a bit of the advice from her letter to "do the things I wanted to do and not be afraid of taking risks." When I first considered enlisting in the military, most of my teachers and extended family advised against it, but I was drawn toward it anyway and leapt in. In college and graduate school, I remained in the reserves, then applied for and was accepted into the officer candidate program where I received a USCG Reserve commission in 1997. I retired in 2009.

Over time, the intensity of my memories of the City of Flowers diminished, but the lessons remained—to trust my instincts, believe in myself, to be free from the need to fit in at any cost. Also, I gradually learned to do as Hope Edelman surmised in *Motherless Daughters*— to let the legacy of losing my mother become a sort of companion to live with, rather than an overarching force to live under. Of course, I still made plenty of mistakes but more easily remembered to regroup and decide to do what is right when a correction was needed.

Many, many years later, after Dad retired and was living in a cottage in the Alaskan woods, I was visiting him and rummaging through some drawers when I found a letter Mom had written to him at the same time she had written our letters. Completely surprised,

I asked if I could read it. He agreed, and I read it aloud. For the first time in decades, we cried. The emotional floodgates finally opened, and we talked about that time, about her, about my year abroad, and about my subsequent choices. I asked him why he waited so long to mourn.

He said, "Well, I had three kids to raise and a job to do. I guess there wasn't time for that."

We allowed the tears and joys and memories to rush through us. These emotions were uncomfortable yet comforting and were soon followed by a strong sense of peace and calm. Hugging Dad, I told him he had done a pretty good job raising his children on his own. Then we cleaned up and went to a church potluck.

Selected Bibliography
(by Theme)

Adventure/Travel

Gilman, Susan Jane. *Undress Me in the Temple of Heaven*. New York: Grand Central Publishing, 2009.

Hansel, Bettina. *The Exchange Student Survival Kit*. Boston: Intercultural Press, 2007. 2nd Edition, 2009.

Miller, Basil. *Patty Lou in the Coast Guard*. Grand Rapids, Michigan: Zondervan Publishing House, 1945.

Paget, Ruth Pennington. *Eating Soup With Chopsticks: Sweet Sixteen in Japan*. New York: iUniverse, Inc., 2003.

Roces, Alfredo and Grace. *Philippines (Culture Shock!).* Portland, Oregon: Graphic Arts Center Publishing Company, 1985. Reprint 2001.

Rotary International Youth Exchange http://www. rotary.org/en/StudentsAndYouth/YouthPrograms/ RotaryYouthExchange.

Schwager, Tina and Michele Schuerger. *Gutsy Girls: Young Women Who Dare.* Minneapolis, Minnesota: Free Spirit Publishing, 1999.

Motherloss/Loss of Parent

Davidman, Lynn. *Motherloss.* Berkeley, California: University of California Press Berkeley and Los Angeles, 2000.

Dennison, Amy, Alice, and David. *Our Dad Died: The True Story of Three Kids Whose Lives Changed.* Minneapolis, Minnesota: Free Spirit Publishing, Inc., 2003.

Edelman, Hope. *Motherless Daughters: The Legacy of Loss.* New York: Bantam Doubleday Dell Publishing Group, Inc., 1994.

Fitzgerald, Helen. *The Grieving Teen.* New York: Simon & Schuster, Inc., 2000.

Welch, Diana, Liz, Amanda, and Dan. *The Kids Are All Right: A Memoir.* New York: Harmony Books, 2009.

Young Adult/Sexuality

Echols, Jennifer. *Going Too Far*. New York: Simon & Schuster, Inc., 2009.

Knowles, Jo. *Jumping Off Swings*. Somerville, Massachusetts: Candlewick Press, 2009.

About the Author

Diane E. Greentree has a bachelor's degree in history from Virginia Wesleyan College and a master's degree in international studies from Old Dominion University. She is retired from the US Coast Guard Reserves. She and her husband, Charter, live in Hawaii with their three children. This is her first book.